This journal belongs to

___
___
___

DRAWING is putting a _LINE_ round an IDEA.
Henri Matisse

IDEAS are the beginning Points of All fortunes.
Napoleon Hill

> A MOMENT'S insight is Sometimes WORTH a life's EXPERIENCE. — Oliver Wendell Holmes

CREATE EVERY DAY

imagine the
IMPOSSIBLE

eureka!

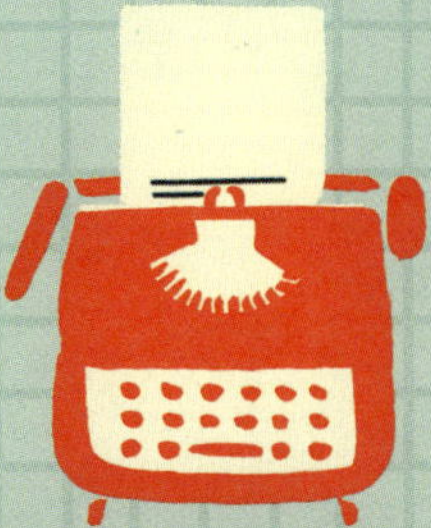

THINK
dream
BELIEVE

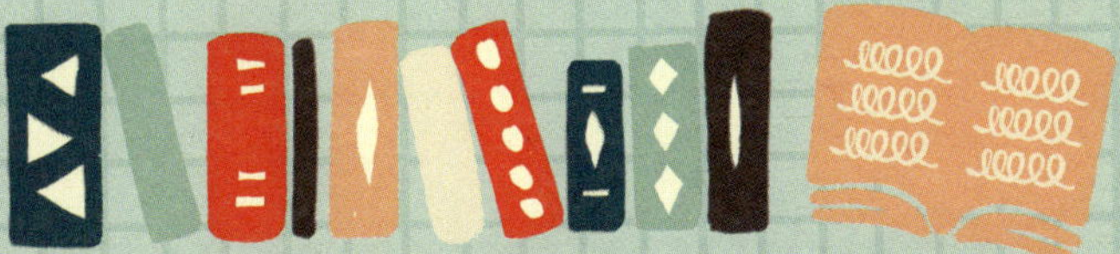

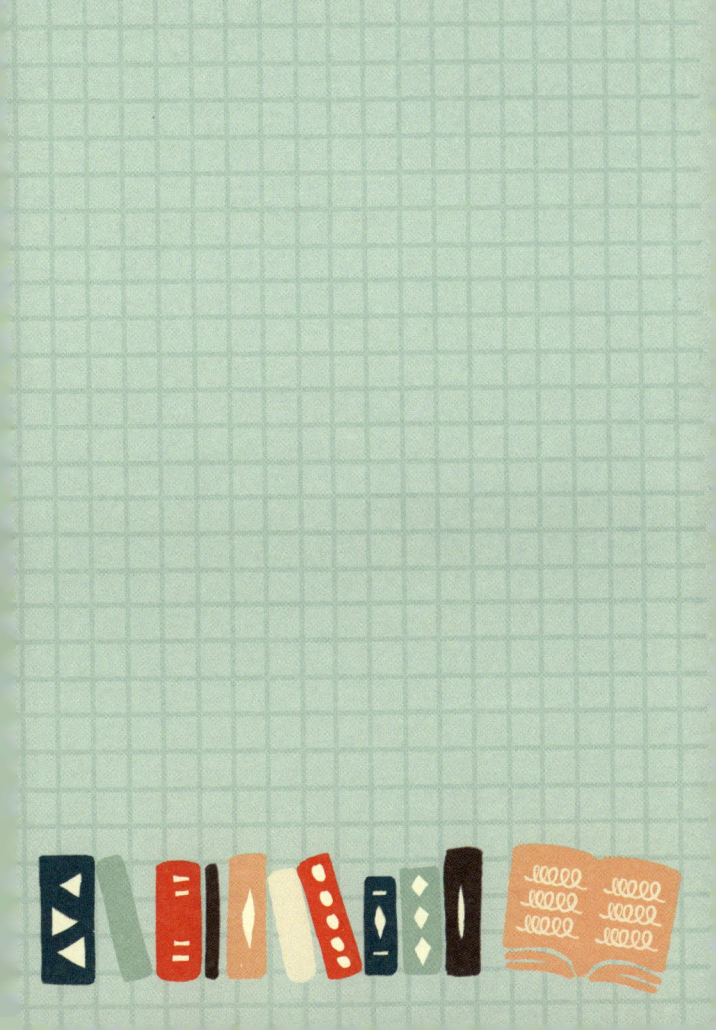

dream

imagine the
IMPOSSIBLE

eureka!

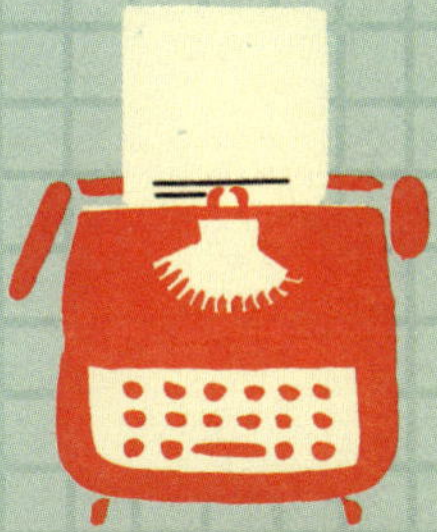

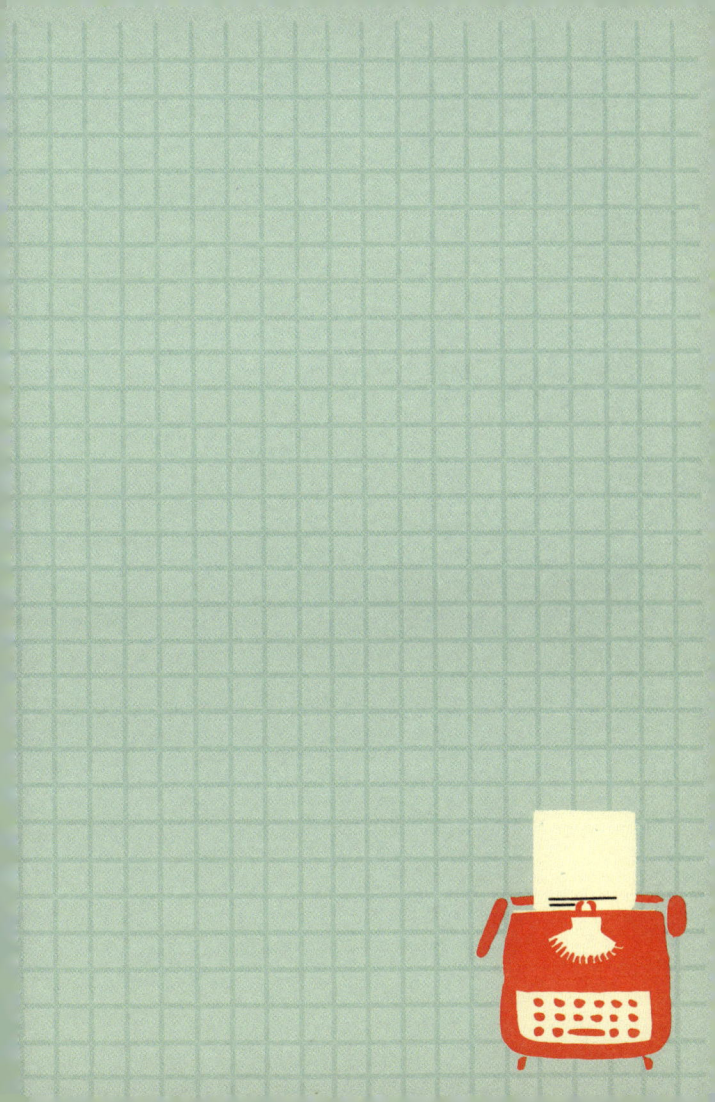

THINK
dream
BELIEVE

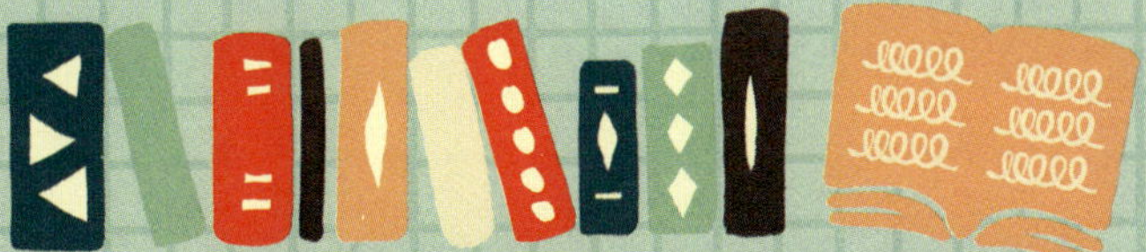

dream

imagine the
IMPOSSIBLE

eureka!

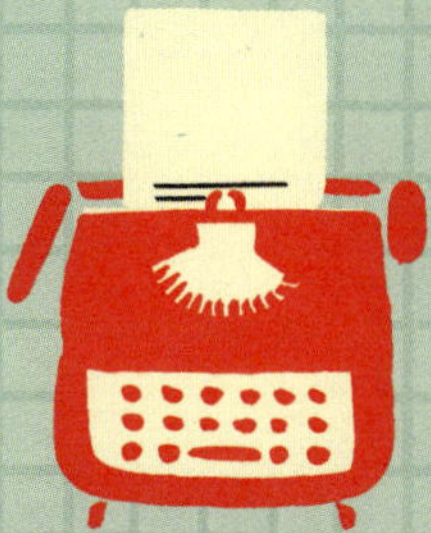

THINK
dream
BELIEVE

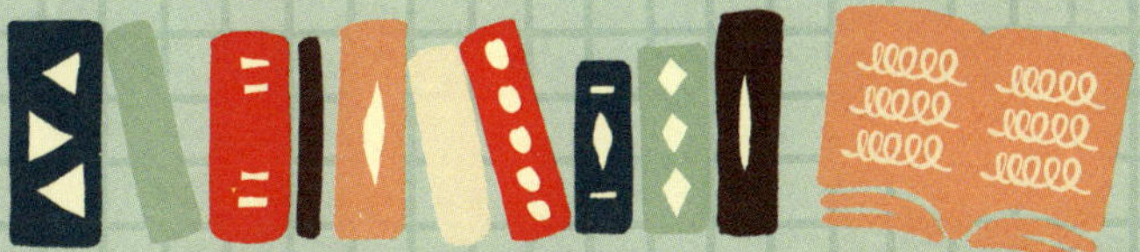

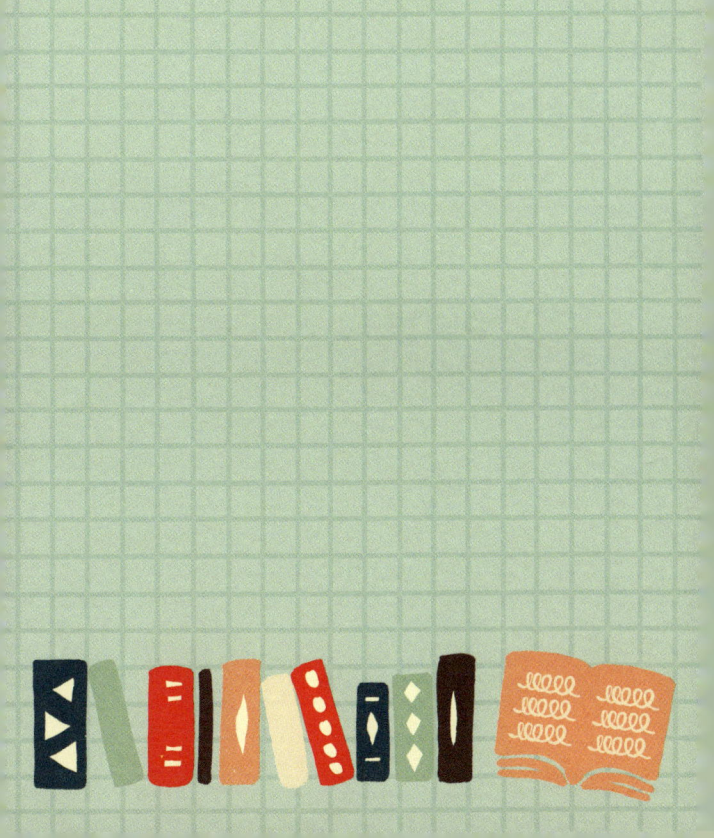

dream

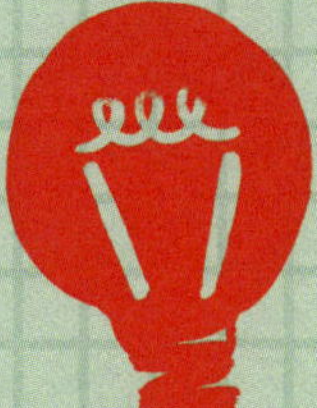

MY IDEAS

Brainstorms

eureka!

eee **MY IDEAS** eee

Brainstorms

MY IDEAS

Brainstorms

My IDEAS

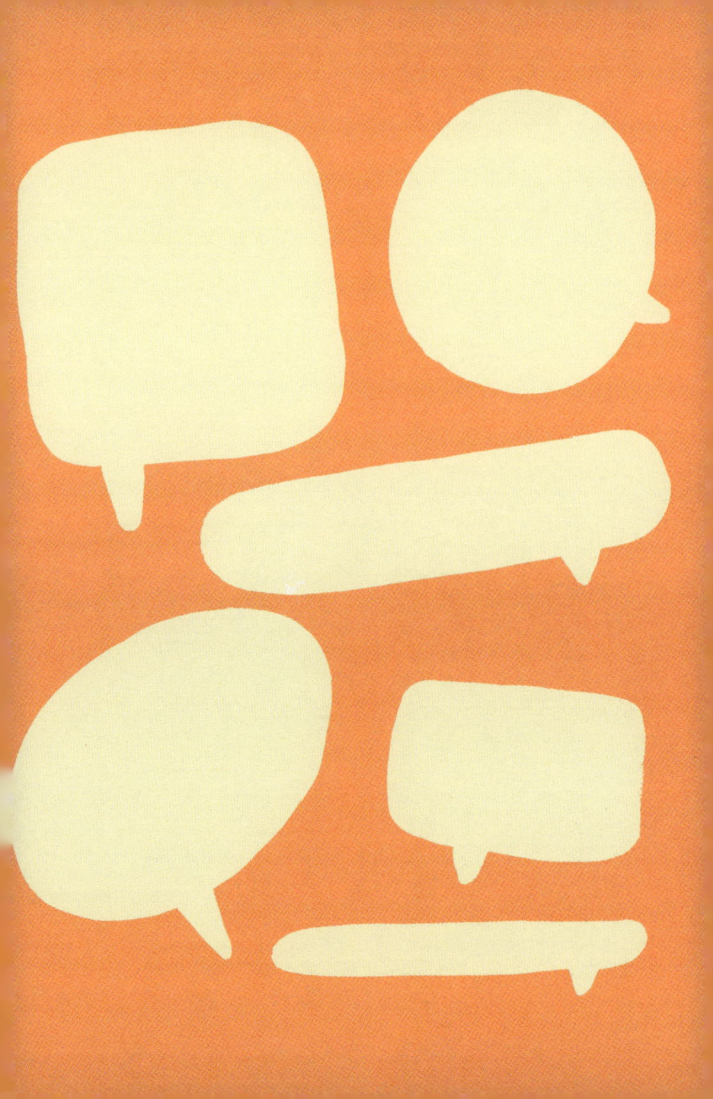

Brainstorms

MY IDEAS

MY IDEAS

Brainstorms

ell MY IDEAS ell

Brainstorms

My IDEAS

Brainstorms

INVENT

My IDEAS

Brainstorms

MY IDEAS

CHECKLIST

IDEAS

PROS	CONS

IDEAS

PROS	CONS

IDEAS

PROS	CONS

IDEAS

PROS	CONS

IDEAS

PROS	CONS

IDEAS

PROS	CONS

IDEAS

PROS	CONS

Notes

CHECKLIST

IDEAS

PROS | CONS

IDEAS

PROS | CONS

IDEAS

PROS	CONS

IDEAS

PROS | CONS

IDEAS

PROS	CONS

IDEAS

PROS | CONS

IDEAS

PROS | CONS

galison

Illustrations © Debbie Powell
www.DebbiePowell.net

New York
GALISON
www.Galison.com

9H7-F5D-3
ISBN 978-0-7353-3689-6

GALISON 28 WEST 44TH STREET · NEW YORK, NY 10036
Designed in the U.S.A. Manufactured in China